Things to Know About Liquidation Preferences in Venture Capital

First published by Kjøller 2023

Disclaimer:

The information contained in this book is provided for general informational purposes only. While every effort has been made to ensure that the information is accurate and up-to-date, The Author makes no representations or warranties of any kind, express or implied, about the completeness, accuracy, reliability, suitability, or availability with respect to the information, products, services, or related graphics contained in the book for any purpose.

The Author disclaims any liability for any loss or damage, including without limitation, indirect or consequential loss or damage, or any loss or damage whatsoever arising from loss of data or profits arising out of, or in connection with, the use of this book.

Readers are solely responsible for determining the appropriateness of the information contained in this book for their specific purposes and should seek professional advice before acting upon any information contained herein. The Author shall not be liable for any damages of any kind arising from the use of this book or the information contained herein.

Table of Contents

Introduction

In the world of venture capital, liquidation preferences are an essential component of investment terms. But what exactly are they? And why are they so important? For entrepreneurs seeking funding or investors seeking to invest in startups, understanding liquidation preferences is crucial.

This book aims to provide a comprehensive glossary of terms related to liquidation preferences in venture capital. From understanding the basics of liquidation preferences to diving into the intricacies of preference stack and participating preferred, this book covers it all. Whether you're an entrepreneur, investor, or simply interested in learning more about venture capital, this book will be a valuable resource for decoding the complex language of liquidation preferences.

Acceleration clauses

Refers to terms that grant investors the right to receive their entire investment back if the startup is acquired before the agreed-upon maturity date. This is to ensure that investors get a fair return on their investment without having to wait for the full term.

Accrued dividends

Refers to unpaid dividends that accumulate and can be paid out upon liquidation or redemption of preferred shares. These dividends are like interest payments and are used to incentivize investors to hold onto their shares for longer periods.

Agreements

Refers to the legally binding documents that govern the terms of the investment. These documents typically include share purchase agreements, investor rights agreements, and articles of association, among others.

Angel investors

Refers to high net-worth individuals who invest in startups in exchange for equity. These investors are typically the first to invest in a company and provide the initial capital needed to get the business off the ground. They often provide mentorship and strategic guidance to the startups they invest in.

Angel round

Refers to the first round of funding that a startup receives from angel investors, typically in exchange for an equity stake. This round often precedes the venture capital rounds and is used to raise the initial capital needed to get the business off the ground.

Anti-dilution protection

Refers to provisions that protect investors from dilution of their ownership in subsequent rounds of funding. This provision is used to maintain the integrity of the initial investment and ensure that investors receive a fair return on their investment.

Anti-dilution provisions

Refers to clauses in investment agreements that protect investors from dilution of their ownership in case of subsequent rounds of funding. These provisions come in two types, full ratchet and weighted average, which protect investors differently based on the nature of the dilution.

Asymmetrical liquidation preferences

Refers to terms that offer different liquidation preferences to different classes of investors. This provision is used when investors have different risk profiles and investment objectives and ensures that each investor is compensated fairly in case of liquidation.

Automatic conversion

Refers to a provision that converts preferred shares into common shares automatically at a specified date or triggering event. This provision is designed to help startups streamline their capital structure and provide an easier path to exit.

Avoidance of liquidation preference stacking

Refers to a term that prevents multiple liquidation preferences from being applied to a single investment. This term ensures that all investors receive an equitable return on their investment and prevents any one investor from receiving a disproportionate return.

Base Case Scenario

The anticipated financial performance of a company without any additional funds from investors or other sources. In venture capital, this scenario is compared to worst-case and best-case scenarios, which help determine the value of a company and the potential returns for investors.

Best-Case Scenario

The most optimistic outcome for a company's financial performance. In venture capital, this scenario is compared to worst-case and base-case scenarios, which help determine the value of a company and the potential returns for investors. The best-case scenario can impact the liquidation preference for investors.

Black-Scholes Model

A mathematical model used to calculate the theoretical value of an option. In venture capital, this model can be used to estimate the value of a company's equity options, which can impact the liquidation preference for investors.

Board Member

An individual elected by shareholders to oversee the activities of a company and make significant decisions. In venture capital, board members may have the power to influence the decision-making process related to liquidation preference, among other important financial matters.

Book Value

The value of a company as recorded in its financial statements. In venture capital, book value can be a useful starting point for determining the appropriate liquidation preference, but other factors such as market conditions and future potential must also be considered.

Break-Even Point

The point at which a company's revenue equals its costs, resulting in neither a profit nor a loss. In venture capital, this is an important metric to consider when evaluating a company's potential for profitability and determining an appropriate liquidation preference.

Bridge Loan

A short-term loan used to finance a company until a larger funding round can be secured. In venture capital, bridge loans are often used to help companies stay afloat until they can reach profitability, which can impact the liquidation preference.

Burn Rate

The rate at which a company is spending its cash reserves. In venture capital, this rate is closely monitored to ensure a company has enough funds to reach its revenue goals and avoid running out of money before achieving profitability.

Business Plan

A detailed document outlining a company's goals, strategies, and financial projections. In venture capital, a strong business plan is crucial to securing funding from investors and can help determine the appropriate liquidation preference for those investments.

Buyout

An acquisition of a company's shares by a larger company or group of investors. In venture capital, the buyout price and terms can impact the liquidation preference for existing investors.

Caps

Caps are a type of liquidation preference that limit the amount of money that preferred shareholders can receive in the event of a sale. This is usually a fixed dollar amount or a percentage of the sale price. Caps are typically used to protect investors from excessive losses, and to ensure that they receive a reasonable return on their investment.

Carve-out

A carve-out is a provision that reserves a certain percentage of the sale proceeds for preferred shareholders in the event of a sale. This is usually a percentage of the total sale price, and is typically reserved for preferred shareholders with liquidation preferences.

Cash-on-cash returns

Cash-on-cash returns are a measure of the return on investment that investors receive in the form of cash payments. This is typically calculated by dividing the cash payout by the amount of investment made, and is used to evaluate the performance of investments over time.

Clawback provisions

Clawback provisions are provisions that allow investors to recover all or part of their investment if certain conditions are met. These provisions are typically used to protect investors from excessively risky investments, and to ensure that they receive a reasonable return on their investment.

Clean-up provisions

Clean-up provisions are provisions that require preferred shareholders to be paid first in the event of a sale or bankruptcy. These provisions are typically used to ensure that preferred shareholders receive their promised payouts before any common shareholders receive theirs.

Control premium

A control premium is a premium paid to the owners of a controlling stake in a company in the event of a sale. This premium is typically paid to incentivize owners to sell their stake, and is designed to offset any potential losses they might incur as a result of the sale.

Control triggers

Control triggers are conditions that must be met before any preferred shareholders can receive their promised payouts. These triggers are typically set to protect investors from excessive losses, and to ensure that they receive a reasonable return on their investment. Some examples of control triggers might include changes in management, significant drops in revenue or profits, or changes in the company's overall strategy.

Conversion preference

Conversion preference is a type of liquidation preference that allows preferred shareholders to convert their preferred shares into common shares. This is typically done to give shareholders more flexibility in how they can participate in the company's growth, and to protect them from losses in the event of a sale.

Conversion ratio

The conversion ratio is a term used to describe the number of shares of preferred stock that can be converted into shares of common stock. In the context of liquidation preferences, the higher the conversion ratio, the better for investors. A higher conversion ratio means that, in the event of a sale, preferred shareholders can convert their shares into common shares, which they can then sell for a higher price than their preferred shares would fetch in a liquidation.

Cumulative dividends

Cumulative dividends are a type of liquidation preference that ensures that preferred shareholders receive a dividend payment before any other shareholders receive one. These dividends are typically set at a fixed rate, and are paid out cumulatively over time. This means that if a dividend is not paid one year, it will accumulate and be paid out in future years.

Debt Financing

Debt financing refers to a funding method in which a company takes out a loan or issues bonds to finance its operations. Debt financing is different from equity financing, which requires selling shares of the company to investors. Unlike in equity financing, investors in debt financing do not have ownership stakes in the company.

Deprioritization

Deprioritization is a common provision in venture capital term sheets that allows for the amendment or reduction of an existing liquidation preference to enable the company to raise new rounds of funding. This provision helps to protect the interests of new investors and reduce the impact of previous investors' liquidation preferences.

Dilution

Dilution refers to the reduction in an individual's ownership percentage of a company's equity as a result of the issuance of new shares to raise capital or stock options given to employees. Dilution can have an impact on liquidation preferences, as it affects the distribution of proceeds from an exit event.

Dividend Preference

Dividend preference is a type of liquidation preference in venture capital that guarantees a specific return to preferred shareholders before any dividends can be paid to common shareholders. Dividend preference is often used in late-stage deals or companies with stable cash flow to provide a steady income stream to investors.

Double-Dip Liquidation Preference

A double-dip liquidation preference in venture capital means that the investors get paid upfront before the common shareholders, just like with a regular liquidation preference. Additionally, after the liquidation preference is paid out, investors can also convert their preferred shares into common shares and receive a pro-rata share of the remaining proceeds. This provision often benefits investors at the expense of common shareholders.

Down-Round

A down-round is a funding round in which a company raises money at a lower valuation than in the previous funding round. Down-rounds are often a red flag for investors as they indicate declining prospects for a company and can significantly dilute existing shareholders. Down-rounds can also trigger ratchet provisions in liquidation preferences, which can increase the investors' payout at the expense of common shareholders.

Downside Protection

Downside protection is one type of liquidation preference in venture capital that guarantees a minimum return to investors in case of a liquidation or exit event with proceeds below the agreed return threshold. It is often used in early-stage deals or businesses with high risk of failure to help investors mitigate risks.

Drag-Along Rights

As a type of liquidation preference in venture capital, drag-along rights is a provision that enables the majority shareholder or investors to force the remaining shareholders to sell their stake in a company at the same terms and conditions as those being offered to the majority shareholders during sale or merger of the business. This provision ensures that all shareholders get equal treatment during an exit event, but it can also limit minority shareholders' control over their investment.

Dual-Class Structure

Dual-class structure is a legal structure in which multiple classes of shares with different voting rights are issued by a company. This structure is more common in early-stage startups, where the founders or major shareholders want to retain control over the company even after raising capital from outside investors.

Due Diligence

Due diligence is the process of conducting an investigation or audit of a company before investing in it. In venture capital, due diligence involves evaluating the target company's financials, management team, market potential, intellectual property, and other relevant factors to determine the risk and potential of the investment.

Early-Stage Investment

An investment in a company during its early stages of development, often when it is still in the concept or prototype phase, with the potential for high returns but also high risks.

Equity

Ownership in a company, often represented by shares or options, that provides investors with a stake in a company and a potential return on their investment.

Escrow Account

A financial account where funds are held by a third party until certain conditions are met, such as achieving a certain milestone, in order to protect the interests of investors.

Excess Liquidation Preference

A feature of preferred stock that guarantees a certain multiple of the initial investment amount to the investor, but any remaining assets will be distributed to other shareholders based on their ownership percentage.

Exit Strategy

A plan that outlines how investors will exit their investment and potentially receive a return on their capital, often through a sale or IPO of the company.

Financial Model

A Financial Model is a tool used by VCs to forecast a startup's potential financial performance. Financial models typically analyze key financial metrics such as revenue, expenses, and cash flow to assess the long-term viability of a company and its ability to provide a return on investment to its investors.

First Refusal Rights

First Refusal Rights are a type of investor protection that give preferred shareholders (VCs) the right to purchase their pro-rata share of any new equity issuances before they are offered to other investors. This protects the VCs from dilution by effectively guaranteeing their percentage ownership in the company.

Follow-On Investment

A Follow-On Investment is a subsequent investment made by a VC firm into one of its portfolio companies. This is typically done to provide additional capital to help the company reach a key milestone or expand its operations.

Forced Conversion

Forced Conversion is a Liquidation Preference that gives VCs the right to convert their preferred shares into common stock upon the occurrence of a specified event, such as an IPO. This converts their equity stake into common stock, which typically has more voting rights and overall more benefits than preferred shares.

Founder Vesting

Founder vesting is a tool that VCs often use to ensure that founders remain committed to their company for an extended amount of time. Founder vesting imposes a vesting schedule that requires founders to earn their equity over time based on their continued involvement with the company. This incentivizes founders to stay with the company, rather than leaving after receiving a large amount of equity.

Founder-Friendly Terms

Founder-friendly terms are rights and protections that VCs provide to founders to ensure they maintain a controlling share of the company. These terms might include blocking rights, which allow founders to veto certain decisions, or drag-along rights, which allow founders to force minority shareholders to accept a deal preferred by the majority.

Full Participation

Full Participation is a type of Liquidation Preference in Venture Capital where the preferred stockholders (VCs) are entitled to a percentage of the proceeds from a liquidity event proportionate to their ownership percentage and then also participate pro-rata with common stockholders in the distribution of the remaining proceeds.

Fund Management Fees

Fund Management Fees are the fees paid by limited partners in a venture capital fund to the general partner for managing the fund. Management fees typically range from 1-2% of the committed capital and are used to cover the operating expenses of the VC firm, such as salaries, office rent, and travel expenses.

Fund Size

The Fund Size is the amount of committed capital that a VC firm has available to invest in startups. The size of a VC fund can range from a few million dollars to billions of dollars. The Fund Size is important because it affects how much money a VC firm can invest into any one company and the number of deals they can make in total.

Fundraising

Fundraising is the process by which a VC firm solicits and raises capital from limited partners for a new investment fund. The process typically involves creating a pitch deck and meeting with potential investors to secure commitments.

Geographic Restrictions

Geographic restrictions are common in venture capital. It means that investors may only fund companies within a certain geographic region. This limitation is done for legal reasons, such as the difference in laws between different countries or because investors may not have the resources to operate globally.

Going Public

Going public refers to the process of a private company becoming a public company. This process usually involves an initial public offering (IPO), where the company sells its shares to the public for the first time.

Good Leaver/Bad Leaver

In venture capital, when an employee leaves the company, they are classified as either a good or bad leaver. A good leaver will typically receive compensation in the form of equity or other benefits, while a bad leaver will typically receive little or no compensation.

Grade a Preferred Stock

Grade A preferred stock is a type of preferred stock that has a higher priority than other types of preferred stock. This type of stock is typically associated with higher yields and lower volatility.

Greenmail

Greenmail is a practice used by some investors where they threaten to buy enough shares of a company to take control of it and then demand that the company buys those shares back at a premium. This practice is considered unethical and is illegal in some jurisdictions.

Gross Revenue-Based Financing

Gross revenue-based financing is a form of financing that is based on a company's revenue. In this type of financing, the investor receives a percentage of the company's revenue until the investor has been paid a predetermined amount. After this, the financing agreement ends.

Growth Equity

Growth equity is a type of financing that is used to help a company grow faster. It is usually provided by private equity firms or venture capital firms that invest in later-stage companies.

Growth Hormones

Growth hormones in venture capital refer to the factors that drive a company's growth. It can include factors like customer acquisition, product development, and scaling.

Growth Rounds

Growth rounds are financing rounds that a company usually undergoes after it has raised seed or series A financing. These rounds are usually in the form of venture capital as companies try to scale their businesses. These rounds are used to help a company expand faster and usually have higher valuations.

Guaranteed Minimum Return

Some investors may require a guaranteed minimum return on their investments, which is called a guaranteed minimum return. This type of investment can provide investors with confidence in their investment, knowing that they will receive a certain amount back regardless of the company's success.

High Water Mark

High water mark refers to the highest value that an investment has achieved, and is used to determine the performance fees earned by a fund manager. In the context of venture capital, the high-water mark is used to ensure that the VC firm only charges a performance fee after the investor has recouped their initial investment.

Hit Rate

Hit rate refers to the percentage of investments made by a venture capital firm that result in successful exits or liquidity events. The hit rate is an important metric for evaluating the performance of a VC firm and is used to determine the fund's overall performance.

Holdback

Holdback is a provision in the investment agreement that allows the investor to hold back a portion of the investment until certain milestones are met. This is often used in venture capital agreements to ensure that the founders are motivated to meet certain performance targets before the investor releases the full amount of the investment.

Hurdle Rate

Hurdle Rate is a minimum rate of return that a venture capital firm expects to earn on its investment before the founders or other investors can start earning profits. This protects the VC firms from investing in risky propositions that have little chance of making money in the long run. The rate is usually calculated as a percentage of the investment amount and is generally around 20-30%.

Hybrid Security

A Hybrid security is a type of security that combines features of equity and debt. This means the investor can receive dividends just like equity shareholders, but also has the option of receiving fixed interest payments like a bondholder. They are used by venture capitalists to reduce risk and maximize potential returns.

Illiquidity Discount

An illiquidity discount is a reduction in the value of an asset due to the difficulty of selling it quickly on the market. In venture capital, illiquidity discounts can be applied to the value of a startup due to the lack of options for selling shares or exiting the investment.

Incremental Liquidation Preference

An incremental liquidation preference is a preference structure where investors have the right to receive additional payments depending on the proceeds of a company's sale or liquidation. This gives priority to investors who have invested larger amounts in a company.

Initial Public Offering (IPO)

An IPO is the first time a company offers its stock to the public. This option can be attractive to investors, as it offers the potential for large returns on their investment. However, in some cases, the liquidation preferences of early investors may be affected by the IPO.

Insolvency

This is a condition where a company cannot pay its debts to creditors when they are due. Insolvency can arise due to several reasons, including poor financial management or a lack of cash flow. In these cases, liquidation may be the only option for a company, which can impact investors according to their liquidation preference.

Internal Rate of Return (IRR)

The IRR is a financial metric used by investors to calculate the profitability of an investment. It takes into account the net present value of future cash flows to determine the return on investment. Investors typically use the IRR to compare different investment opportunities and assess their risk tolerance.

Investment Horizon

The investment horizon refers to the period of time for which an investor expects to hold their investment. It is typically determined by the investor's long-term financial goals and risk tolerance. In venture capital, the investment horizon can be several years, during which the investor expects to see a return on their investment or exit the investment.

Investment Valuation

Investment valuation is the process of estimating the value of an investment, such as a company or stock. In venture capital, investment valuation can be complex due to the uncertainty surrounding the future success of a startup. Liquidation preferences may also affect the valuation of an investment.

Investor Preference

This is the amount of money that investors receive from the proceeds of a company's sale or liquidation before any other shareholders are paid out. This ensures that investors recoup their initial investment, and is often used to reflect their level of risk in financing the company's growth.

Investor Rights Agreement

An investor rights agreement is a legal agreement between investors and a company that outlines the rights of investors, such as the right to receive regular financial reports and vote on important company decisions. The agreement can also outline the liquidation preferences of investors.

Investor Waterfall

The investor waterfall is the priority order and percentage of distributions made to investors and shareholders from a company's profits or liquidation proceeds. The investor waterfall typically determines the proportion of money each investor or class of investors receives in relation to their initial investment.

J Curve

J Curve is a measure of the performance of a private investment fund over time. It resembles the letter J as it initially dips below the starting point and then gradually rises. This is due to the initial investment in the fund being higher than the returns received in the early years of the fund, with the returns gradually increasing over time. This concept is relevant to liquidation preferences as it demonstrates the importance of considering the time horizon of the investment.

J-Curve Effect

The J-curve effect is a phenomenon where the returns of an investment decrease initially and then improve over time. This effect can be relevant to liquidation preferences as it underlines the importance of considering the long-term returns of an investment, rather than just the initial liquidation preferences.

Joint and Several Liability

Joint and several liability is a legal concept that applies to multiple parties who are jointly liable for a debt or obligation. Each party is individually responsible for the full amount of the debt, and the creditor can choose to pursue any or all of the parties for payment. In the context of liquidation preferences, joint and several liability can be relevant in cases where multiple investors hold preferred shares and have different liquidation preferences.

Joint Obligation

Joint obligation refers to a legal obligation shared by two or more parties. In the context of liquidation preferences, joint obligation can be relevant in cases where multiple investors have invested in a company and hold preferred shares with different liquidation preferences. The company may have a joint obligation to fulfill these preferences, which can be challenging to manage in the event of liquidation.

Joint Ventures

Joint ventures refer to a business arrangement where two or more parties come together for a specific project or purpose. Joint ventures are often used in the context of venture capital as a way for investors to pool their resources and expertise to leverage each other's strengths. In terms of liquidation preferences, joint ventures can provide a mechanism for sharing any potential losses or gains that may result from the venture.

Jointly Held

Jointly held refers to the ownership of an asset by two or more parties where they each have an equal interest in the property. Jointly held assets can be relevant to liquidation preferences because they can complicate the liquidation process in the event of a partnership dissolution or asset sale.

Judgmental Adjustment

Judgmental adjustment refers to a situation where an investor adjusts the valuation of an investment based on their own judgment, rather than on any objective data. This can be relevant to liquidation preferences as investors may use judgmental adjustment to account for uncertain factors, such as the timing or likelihood of future events.

Jump on Exit

Jump on exit is a provision in a shareholder agreement that allows certain shareholders to convert their preferred shares into common shares in the event of an exit, such as a sale or merger. The conversion allows the shareholders to participate in any potential upside that may result from the exit. This provision can potentially dilute the ownership of common shareholders.

Junior

In the context of liquidation preferences, junior refers to a class of preferred shares that rank lower in priority to a senior class. Junior preferred shares are typically offered to new investors and have a lower liquidation preference. In the event of liquidation, holders of junior preferred stock will only receive payment after senior preferred stockholders have been paid in full.

Just-in-Time Financing

Just-in-time financing refers to a type of financing where funds are raised only when they are needed. This approach is often used in startup companies as it allows them to raise capital without giving up excessive equity or control. Just-in-time financing can be beneficial in terms of liquidation preferences as it allows companies to minimize their dilution and retain more control over the company.

Kalanick clause

A clause in a contract that prohibits certain individuals from holding executive positions in a startup. This was famously used in the resignations of Uber CEO Travis Kalanick and other executives amid allegations of misconduct.

Key Deal Terms

The primary terms of an investment that are negotiated between investors and startup founders. This can include liquidation preferences, valuation, board composition, and more.

Key man insurance

An insurance policy that protects the investment in a startup by compensating investors for losses incurred by the unexpected departure or death of a key member of the team. This is important in venture capital, as investors are often heavily reliant on the success of the startup's management team.

Key Non-Dilutive Financing

A form of financing that does not require the dilution of a startup's equity. This can include grants, subsidies, or tax credits provided by government or private entities. Investors may view the availability of non-dilutive financing as a positive sign for a startup, as it can indicate stability and government support.

Kicker

A clause in a contract that rewards select investors in a liquidation event by providing them with an additional payout or equity stake. This can be an important factor in negotiating liquidation preferences, as a kicker can incentivize investors to take on more risk in funding a startup.

Kick-out rights

A provision that allows investors to remove a member of a startup's board of directors or management team if they believe that person is not acting in the best interest of the company. This can be a valuable tool for investors to protect their investment.

Know-how

The specific skills and knowledge possessed by a startup's founders or management team that give them a competitive advantage over other companies in their industry. Investors often look for companies with strong know-how in order to increase the likelihood of a successful exit.

KPIs

Key Performance Indicators, which are metrics used to assess the success or failure of a startup. Common KPIs in venture capital include revenue growth, customer acquisition, and user engagement.

Kroll report

A comprehensive report that assesses potential risks associated with a startup, including any past legal issues, regulatory violations, or financial instability. Investors often commission Kroll reports as part of their due diligence process.

KYC

Know Your Customer, a regulatory requirement that financial institutions must abide by in order to prevent money laundering and fraud. This is relevant in venture capital as investors often need to perform thorough due diligence on startups before investing in them in order to make sure they are a legitimate business.

Lead Investor

A venture capitalist who takes the primary role in a funding round and takes charge of the negotiations with the company. They may also take a board seat, provide follow-on financing, and assist with the company's growth strategy.

Leverage

A term that refers to the use of borrowed funds for investment purposes. Leverage can magnify the returns but also increases the risk of losses. In venture capital, leverage can come from debt financing or the use of convertible securities.

Life Cycle

It is a term that refers to the stages of a company's development, from its formation to its exit. The life cycle includes different phases, such as seed, early-stage, growth, and maturity, each with its funding needs, risks, and opportunities. Venture capital firms typically focus on specific stages of the life cycle and provide capital and support to companies at those stages.

Limited Partners

They are investors in a venture fund who provide the capital but have limited participation in the management of the portfolio companies. Also, they are entitled to receive a portion of the profits if the fund is successful.

Liquidated Damages

A term used to refer to contractual provisions that specify damages that one party will pay to the other in case of a breach. In venture capital, liquidated damages are sometimes used to compensate investors for losses resulting from fraud or misrepresentation by the company's management.

Liquidation Event

It is an occurrence that can trigger the liquidation of a company, such as a bankruptcy, acquisition, or merger. When a liquidation event occurs, the proceeds are used to pay off the company's liabilities, and the remaining funds are distributed to the equity holders based on their liquidation preferences.

Liquidation Multiple

It is a term that specifies the multiple of a liquidation preference that investors are entitled to receive before the common shareholders receive any proceeds. For example, if the liquidation preference is 1.5x, the investor will be entitled to receive 1.5 times their initial investment before any other shares are paid out.

Liquidation Preference

A term that refers to an investor's right to receive their initial investment before any other equity holders in case of a company's liquidation. This preference can be either participating or non-participating, and it can also be capped or uncapped.

Liquidation Waterfall

It is a process used to distribute proceeds among different classes of investors in a specific order during a company's liquidation. The sequence of payments is defined in the company's investment agreement, which determines the order of preference, and the percentage of the distribution each class is entitled to receive.

Lock-up Period

It is a period during which certain shareholders, such as insiders or early investors, are prohibited from selling their shares in a company. This restriction can be part of an IPO or a merger agreement and can last from a few months to a year or more.

Mandatory Conversion

This is a clause in the to preferred share agreement that forces the conversion of preferred shares to common shares after a certain period of time or upon the occurrence of a specific event.

Market Capitalization

This is the value of the company obtained by multiplying the number of outstanding shares by the current market price of these shares. This value is used to determine the valuation of the company and the price of its shares.

Maturity Date

This is the date where the investors' right to convert their preferred shares to common shares or redeem their preferred shares for their investment amount expires. If this date is not defined, the company might be forced to redeem the preferred shares at any time, which could be detrimental to the company.

Mezzanine Financing

This is a type of financing where companies issue preferred shares that are subordinate to senior debt but senior to common shares. This financing is usually done when the company is about to go public or get acquired, and is used to bridge the gap between the last round of financing and the exit event.

Milestone Financing

This is a type of financing where companies receive funds in stages as they achieve certain milestones. This financing helps the investors monitor and control the progress of the company and reduce the risk of failure.

Multiple Liquidation Preferences

This is a type of liquidation preference where investors are entitled to receive back their investment amount along with additional returns upon exit of the company, before any other class of shares can receive any proceeds. For example, if an investor has a 2x multiple liquidation preference and invested $1 million, he would get back $2 million before any other shareholder gets any amount.

Negotiated Preferences

Negotiated preferences refer to customized preferences that have been established during negotiations between the investor and the company. This type of preference can vary depending on the bargaining power of each party involved, resulting in different liquidation preferences for different investors.

Non-Participating Preferred Stock

This is a type of stock that gives its holder the right to receive their initial investment back in the event of a liquidation before common stockholders receive any distribution. The preferred stockholders are not entitled to participate in any remaining proceeds after receiving their initial investment back.

Option acceleration

A provision that accelerates the vesting of stock options if specific events occur, such as a change of control or acquisition. The acceleration provision ensures that employees are not left with unvested options in the event of a significant change in the company's control or ownership.

Option agreement

A contract between an employer and an employee that outlines the terms of the stock options being offered. Among other details, the agreement typically includes the number of shares being granted, the exercise price, and the exercise period.

Option exercise price

The amount an employee must pay to buy one share of their awarded options. The exercise price is usually set at the company's common stock FMV on the day of the grant.

Option expiration date

The date by which the employee must use their options. If the employee does not exercise their options by this date, they will lose the right to do so.

Option pool

A term used to describe the portion of a startup's equity set aside for future employee stock options. Option pool is a significant factor in determining pre-money valuations during funding rounds. Investors tend to offer smaller investments if there is inadequate provision for option pool in a startup.

Option pool shuffle

The act of reallocating the option pool before a new funding round. The option pool shuffle is done to maintain the company's equity structure and ensure that there are enough shares available to the new employees.

Option repricing

It is the process of lowering the exercise price of an employee's stock options. A common scenario for repricing is when the stock of a company has dropped or is likely to fall, making the options out of the money. Repricing is used to maintain morale among employees by ensuring their incentive stock options are still valuable.

Option vesting

The process whereby an employee gains the right to use their options over time. Vesting periods are typically measured in years or months and rely on the employee staying with the company until the vesting date is reached.

Out-of-cycle financing

It refers to the process of obtaining funding from venture capitalists outside the typical funding cycles. Such a financial arrangement often involves the sale of preferred stock with liquidation preferences.

Overhang

It is the difference between the total shares outstanding and the fully diluted shares. The overhang is significant because it represents the pool of shares eligible to be granted as employee stock options.

Pari Passu

Pari passu is a Latin expression that means "equal footing". In the context of venture capital, it refers to the concept that investors should be treated equally with respect to their liquidation preferences and other rights and privileges. This means that investors with pari passu rights would receive the same treatment in terms of payouts and other benefits, regardless of their position in the capital structure.

Participating Preferred Stock

Participating preferred stock is a type of preferred stock that grants investors the right to receive additional proceeds on top of their initial investment. In exchange for this preference, participating preferred stockholders typically give up their right to vote on company decisions.

Participation Rights

Participation rights are a type of liquidation preference that enable investors to receive a pro-rata share of remaining proceeds after receiving their initial preference. Essentially, when a company is sold or goes public, investors with participation rights can receive an additional return on top of their initial investment based on their percentage ownership of the company.

Pay-to-Play Provision

A pay-to-play provision is a stipulation in a financing agreement that requires investors to continue investing in a company in order to maintain their equity stake. If an investor fails to meet the requirement, they may lose their existing equity or have their shares converted to a lower class of stock.

Preferred Return

A preferred return is the minimum rate of return on an investment that investors must receive before any other profits are distributed. In the context of venture capital, preferred returns are often associated with convertible debt, which offers a fixed interest rate that must be paid before investors can convert their debt into equity.

Preferred Stock

Preferred stock is a type of ownership in a company that generally offers higher dividends and priority in liquidation than common stock. This priority is called the liquidation preference, and can vary depending on the terms of the preferred stock agreement.

Pro Rata

Pro rata refers to the proportional allocation of something based on ownership or investment. In the context of venture capital, pro rata rights allow existing investors to maintain their ownership percentage in a company when new funding rounds occur.

Protective Provisions

Protective provisions are clauses in a financing agreement that enable investors to protect their rights and interests by requiring company management to seek investor approval before making certain decisions or taking certain actions.

Purchase Agreement

A purchase agreement is a legal contract between a buyer and seller outlining the terms of a transaction. In the context of venture capital, purchase agreements typically involve the acquisition of preferred stock or convertible debt in exchange for an investment.

Put Option

A put option is a financial contract that gives the holder the right, but not the obligation, to sell an asset at a specified price before a certain date. In the context of venture capital, put options are sometimes used to protect investors in the event of a down round, enabling them to sell their shares back to the company at a predetermined price.

Qualified Financing

A financing round that meets the specific criteria which is set by investors to establish a benchmark to trigger the next investment in the funding cycle.

Qualitative Preferences

Liquidation preferences in venture capital that are subject to negotiations with investors based on factors such as market conditions, business potential, and competition. This type of preference is not typically defined by a specific numerical value.

Quantitative Preferences

Liquidation preferences in venture capital that are defined by a specific numerical value, usually expressed as a multiple of the investment amount. This value is fixed and non-negotiable.

Quasi-Dilution

The reduction of the value of the shares and ownership of the outstanding shares. This can occur in companies when management issues new shares, diluting the value of the current stockholders.

Quasi-equity

A form of instrument that possesses both characteristics of equity and debt. Quasi-equity has the potential to serve as an attractive financing option for companies that may not have the creditworthiness to approach traditional lenders.

Quasi-Reorganization

A process where a company can restructure itself while avoiding the legal process of bankruptcy. This process may allow companies to minimize losses and maintain control.

Quasi-Successor

A provision that is commonly used in fund structures in venture capital. It refers to the situation where the general partner forms a new fund with similar strategy and typically uses a portion (or all) of the performance fees generated by the prior fund.

Quick-Flip Provision

This provision allows the preferred investors to sell their shares to the buyer at the same price the company is sold. This can create an incentive for the preferred investors to sell their shares more quickly.

Quiet Liquidation Preference

A type of liquidation preference in venture capital that allows a preferred investor to receive a fixed return before any distributions are made to other investors. This preference does not grant any participation rights in the equity of the company.

Quorum

A minimum number or proportion of shareholders required for a meeting on liquidation preferences in venture capital to be valid. This is usually determined by the company's bylaws or the applicable laws.

Redemption Right

A Redemption Right is an investor's right to force the company to buy back its preferred shares at a predetermined price. This helps investors protect their investments in case the company experiences financial difficulty or does not meet certain performance standards. Redemption Rights can be beneficial to investors but can also limit the company's ability to reinvest in itself.

Return Multiple

The Return Multiple determines how much an investor will receive in the event of a sale or liquidation of the company. This multiple is typically equal to the amount of the investment plus a predetermined return percentage. For example, a Return Multiple of 2x means that the investor will receive twice the amount of their original investment.

Reverse Vesting

Reverse Vesting is a mechanism that ensures that founders and employees earn their equity over time. This means that if a founder or employee leaves the company before a certain time period, they forfeit a portion of their shares.

Secondary Liquidation Preference

A secondary liquidation preference means that the VCs will receive their liquidation preference only after certain minimum returns have been paid to other classes of shareholders. The secondary liquidation preference can be used to align the interests of the VC investors and the common shareholders and to ensure that the VCs do not take all the proceeds in a liquidation event.

Senior Liquidation Preference

Senior liquidation preference means that the VC investors will be paid before any other class of shareholders in a liquidation event. The senior liquidation preference amount is typically set at a multiple of the initial investment to ensure that the VCs receive a minimum return on investment if the startup is liquidated.

Seniority

Seniority refers to the order in which different classes of shareholders are paid in the event of a liquidation event. Senior shareholders are paid first, followed by junior shareholders. Seniority can be determined by different factors, such as date of investment, class of shares, and liquidation preference amount. Seniority is an important factor in determining the distribution of proceeds amongst shareholders in a liquidation event.

Series A

Series A is the first round of VC funding for a startup. The terms of the Series A round, including the liquidation preference, are typically negotiated between the VC investors and the startup management team. The Series A round is often seen as a critical milestone for startups and can set the tone for subsequent rounds of funding.

Sharerun

Share run is the process of distributing proceeds amongst shareholders in a liquidation event. The share run typically follows a predetermined order based on the seniority, subordination, and liquidation preference of each class of shares, as well as any contractual obligations or agreements between the shareholders.

Stacked vs non-stacked

A stacked liquidation preference means that the VC investors will receive their liquidation preference first before the common shareholders receive any proceeds. In contrast, a non-stacked liquidation preference means that the VC investors and the common shareholders will receive their proceeds together, after which the investors will receive their liquidation preference. Whether the liquidation preference is stacked or non-stacked can make a significant difference in the distribution of proceeds among shareholders.

Startups

Startups are typically early-stage companies that are in the process of developing and commercializing innovative products or services. Startups often require significant amounts of funding to support their growth and development, and they frequently turn to VCs as a source of funding.

Strike Price

The strike price is the price at which VCs purchase their preferred shares. The strike price is usually set at a premium to the common share price to compensate VCs for the additional preferences and rights attached to the preferred shares. The strike price can be used to determine the liquidation preference amount and the potential return on investment for the VCs in a liquidation event.

Subordinated

A subordinated liquidation preference means that the VC investors will receive their liquidation preference only after the common shareholders receive certain minimum returns. Subordination can be used to align the interests of the VCs and the common shareholders and to ensure that the VCs do not take all the proceeds in a liquidation event.

Sumitomo Mitsui

Sumitomo Mitsui is a Japanese VC fund that specializes in investing in early-stage companies. Sumitomo Mitsui has a global presence and invests in a wide range of industries, including IT, healthcare, and energy. VCs such as Sumitomo Mitsui play an important role in providing funding and support to startups, and they can help drive innovation and economic growth.

Term

Total Liquidation Preference (TLP)

Ultra Vires

This term refers to actions or activities undertaken by a company that are beyond the scope of its legal authority. For example, a company may attempt to issue securities or make investments in a manner that exceeds its legal limits. In the case of liquidation preferences, the legality of the actions of a company can impact the validity of the preferences.

Unanimous Consent

This term refers to a requirement that all parties involved in a decision must agree before the decision can be made. In the context of liquidation preferences, unanimous consent can be required before changes to the preferred stock terms and conditions can be made. This requirement can protect the preferred stockholders' rights and ensure that their interests are considered in the decision-making process.

Unconverted Preferred Stock

This term refers to the type of preferred stock that can be converted into common stock. The conversion takes place at the time of the liquidity event, such as an IPO or sale of the company. In exchange for the conversion, the preferred stockholders may receive a more significant amount of equity than other shareholders. This conversion can impact liquidation preferences since the preferred stockholders' claims may lower or have a more significant impact on the distribution of assets.

Underlying Shares

This term refers to the common or preferred stock that lies behind the convertible securities, such as convertible bonds or preferred stock. These underlying shares are the shares that are received once the conversion process takes place. Liquidation preferences typically refer to the value of preferred stock, but the value of the underlying shares can impact the amount of the liquidation preference.

Underwater

This term refers to a situation in which the value of an asset falls below the purchase price. For example, if a venture capital firm invests in a company and the company's valuation declines, the preferred stock that the firm holds may be considered "underwater." This situation can impact liquidation preferences since the preferred stockholders may receive a lower payout due to the lower value of the company.

Unfunded Commitment

This term refers to the agreements that venture capital firms and limited partners make to commit capital. However, this commitment does not have cash behind it. This type of commitment allows venture capital firms to be flexible with the amount of money they invest in a company. Therefore, the company may not receive the full amount of funding that was originally promised. This type of commitment is common in the early stages of investment, when a company is not yet ready to receive a large amount of capital.

Unicorn

This term refers to a startup company that has achieved a valuation of $1 billion or more. Unicorns are rare in the venture capital industry, and they often capture the attention of investors and the media. Liquidation preferences for unicorns are typically more complex than for other startups, given the larger amount of capital involved. The unicorn status indicates a high level of potential for the company, which can have implications for its liquidation preferences.

Unsecured Debt

This term refers to a type of debt that is not secured by collateral. In the context of venture capital investments, unsecured debt may be used as a way for a company to receive capital without diluting their equity. Unsecured debt can be converted into equity at a later point, but it typically has a lower priority compared to preferred stock when it comes to distributing assets during a liquidation event.

Upper Tier Investor

This term refers to the investors in a syndicate who hold the senior-most shares in a preferred stock. They are the first group of shareholders to receive payments from the liquidation event. Typically, upper-tier investors are institutional investors or venture capital firms that can invest significant amounts of money in a company. They have greater negotiating power compared to lower-tier investors in the preferred stock. The terms and conditions of their investment can have a significant impact on the liquidation preferences.

Upside Participation

This term refers to the provision within a preferred stock that allows for the preferred stockholder to participate in the upside of a company's performance. In other words, when the company performs well, the preferred stockholders receive a larger payout than they would have without upside participation. This provision can impact liquidation preferences, as it can adjust the distribution of assets based on the performance of the company.

Validity Period

The length of time that liquidation preferences are applicable, usually specified in the terms of the agreement. This can be for a set period or until certain conditions are met, such as a successful IPO or acquisition.

Valuation

The process of determining the value of a company or investment opportunity. This is a crucial factor in negotiating liquidation preferences.

Valuation Cap

A stipulation in the terms of a convertible note or SAFE that limits the maximum valuation of the company when the debt converts into equity.

Venture Capital

Funds provided to early-stage, high-growth companies by investors in exchange for equity in the company.

Venture Capitalist

The individual or firm providing venture capital funds to startups in exchange for equity in the company.

Venture Debt

A form of financing provided to startups that allows them to acquire capital without giving up equity or control. This type of financing typically has higher interest rates and shorter terms than traditional loans.

Vesting

The process by which an employee earns the right to own stock options or other equity-based compensation over a period of time, usually tied to their length of employment.

Vintage Year

The year in which a venture capital fund is established and begins investing in startups. This can impact the fund's overall performance based on economic conditions and market trends at the time.

Volume Discount

A financial incentive offered by venture capitalists to entice startups to give them preferred stock, usually a discount on the purchase price.

Voting Rights

The right of a preferred stock holder to vote in company matters, usually pertaining to electing board members or approving major company changes.

Walk-away rights

A clause in a shareholder agreement that allows an investor to withdraw from the investment or exit a funding round if certain conditions are not met. Walk-away rights can be used to protect investors from unforeseen events or changes in the company's business model.

Warrant

A financial instrument that gives the holder the right to purchase a certain number of shares at a specified price within a specific timeframe. Warrants are often used as an incentive for investors to participate in funding rounds, as they offer the potential for greater returns if the company is successful.

Warrant coverage

The percentage of a company's outstanding shares that are covered by warrants. Warrant coverage can be an important factor in determining the potential dilution of existing shareholders, as the holders of warrants have the right to purchase additional shares at a set price.

Waterfall structure

A term used to describe the distribution of proceeds from a successful liquidation event such as a sale or IPO. The proceeds are distributed based on a predetermined order of priority, with liquidation preferences being given to preferred stockholders before common stockholders receive any proceeds. The distribution then flows downward in a "waterfall" manner until all parties have received their fair share.

Weighted-average anti-dilution protection

A clause in a company's bylaws or shareholder agreement that protects investors from dilution by adjusting their ownership percentage to reflect new share issuances at a lower price than the investors' original investment. The adjustment is calculated based on the weighted average of the old and new share prices.

White paper

A detailed report that outlines a company's technology, product, or business model. White papers are often used to promote the company to investors, customers, or potential partners, and can be a useful tool for educating people about the company's offerings.

Wind-down period

A period of time after a company has decided to shut down its operations, during which the company liquidates its assets and pays off any outstanding debts or obligations. The wind-down period can vary depending on the complexity of the company's operations and the amount of assets that need to be liquidated.

Working capital

A measure of a company's liquidity, calculated by subtracting its current liabilities from its current assets. In venture capital, working capital can be an important factor in determining a company's ability to sustain its operations, as it provides a measure of the company's ability to meet short-term financial obligations.

Working group

A group of investors or stakeholders who work together to achieve a specific goal, such as developing a new product or service or raising funds for the company. Working groups can be an effective way to pool resources and expertise to achieve a common objective.

Write-off

The process of removing an asset from a company's financial statement because it is considered to have no value. In venture capital, write-offs are often necessary when companies fail to achieve their goals or go bankrupt, and are recorded as a loss for the investors.

Y Combinator

Y Combinator is a leading startup accelerator that offers investment, mentorship, and shared workspace for early-stage companies. With a community of seasoned investors, founders, and mentors, Y Combinator's program is beneficial for startups looking to secure funding and grow their businesses through a network of industry peers.

Yahoo Moment

A term used to describe a situation where an investor stands to receive more from liquidation preference than their actual percentage of ownership due to a company's poor financial performance. This can occur when a preferred stock has significant liquidation preferences, and common stock lacks such provisions.

Year-to-Date (YTD)

Year-to-date is a calculation that tells investors how much a stock or other asset has progressed since the beginning of the calendar year. YTD returns are useful for measuring changes in asset values over a particular period and play a critical role in determining the performance of investment portfolios.

Yield Curve

The line on a graph that shows the relationship between yields and maturity dates for a set of fixed-income stocks or bonds over a specified period. When yields are high, yields curve upwards, indicating that investors require more significant risk premiums. Conversely, when yields are low or in decline, the yield curve slopes downwards, indicating a bearish outlook for investors.

Yield Protection

This is an essential clause in venture capitalist contracts that secures a minimum Annual Percentage Rate (APR) return paid out to the investor before any dividends or profits are incurred by the startup. A critical aspect of liquidation preferences, yield protection is used to reduce losses and protect investors from poor investment returns.

Yield Ratio

The investment return estimate divided by the initial investment amount. A yield ratio can help venture capitalists calculate equity returns across investments and determine which investments are providing the highest yields. As a ratio, the yield ratio is a percentage, which means investors can use it to gauge performance easily.

Yield Spread

The gap between two types of fixed income securities, including bonds, notes, and Treasury bills, with different maturities, risks, and interest rates. The Yield spread is an instrumental tool for venture capitalists to understand the difference between the returns on different asset classes and their subsequent risk profiles.

Yield to Maturity

Yield to maturity calculates an estimated return on a bond's full face value, assuming it's purchased at the current market price and held until here maturity date. In cases where startup bonds are released to venture capitalists, yield to maturity can help investors understand the real worth of their investment.

Young Firm Effect

The Young Firm Effect is a concept that states that smaller firms are better positioned to outperform larger ones. Research indicates that small local startups are most likely to sustainably grow over larger multinational corporations. As a result, the venture capitalist has a higher chance of achieving higher ROI from startup equity compared to other traditional investments such as blue-chip stocks and real estate.

Young Venture

Companies that are just starting but have shown potential in their industry are considered young ventures. These firms have minimal assets, limited track records, and high degrees of uncertainty which can attract investors looking for high-risk high-reward opportunities.